BRITISH SAMPLERS

BRITISH SAMPLERS

by

MARY EIRWEN JONES

B.T. Batsford Ltd,
London

ISBN 0 7134 5634 5

Printed and bound in Great Britain by
Anchor Brendon Ltd, Tiptree, Essex
for the publishers
B.T. Batsford Ltd
4 Fitzhardinge Street
London W1H 0AH

The front cover shows an exceptionally fine sampler of 1853, with a central motif
of a sailing ship. Double-meshed canvas embroidered with wool in cross stitch.
Size 27 in. square. *(Carmarthen Museum)*

Frontispiece.

TABLE OF CONTENTS

LIST OF ILLUSTRATIONS

Introduction

In its origin a sampler was an example or sample of stitches used in embroidery. The first samplers were probably worked by adults but later a sampler came to denote work done by children and it evolved from a pattern of stitches to a testimonial of juvenile skill in embroidery. Known by various names such as "exampler", "Samplaire", "sam-cloth", the sampler was in foundation a pattern book in the form of a piece of linen on to which new patterns or designs, new, stitches and colour combinations were worked.

In his "History of the Horn Book", Tuer declared that the purpose of the sampler was akin to that of the horn book in that it served to teach letters and numerals as well as stitches. He held that the sampler taught "letters and stitches at one stroke". Credence is given to this theory by the fact that the alphabet is a very usual phenomenon on a child's sampler. The primary purpose of a sampler, however, was probably the teaching of *stitches*, the young worker being already familiar with the sequence of the alphabet.

Dexterity with the needle was considered all important in a woman's education in Britain up to and well into the Machine Age. The popularity of embroidery and of fine needlework was established in the country during the 15th to the 17th centuries and the sampler itself was one of the most popular forms of needlework for any new and attractive stitches or patterns were entered upon it. On examining the old samplers with their intricate and beautiful embroidery, one sees that years of painstaking labour must have been spent on them. It is more than likely that young eye-sight was more than half-ruined by the minute, meticulous work.

As pattern books, these samplers were a necessity in decades when clothes, both masculine and feminine, showed a luxurious wealth of embroidery. Needlework was an every-day art and both the lady in her castle and the peasant woman in her cottage aimed at perfection with her needle. The furnishings of the house, window and bed hangings, caskets, cushions, pictures and books were all embellished with the needle. Interspersed through British history have been phases when a simple age was introduced. Among such was that when the Puritans were supreme but fine needlework was still fostered. Again, the sampler had a utilitarian aspect for the ornamental alphabet and numerals which it displayed had their purpose for the marking and identification of linen by hand was necessary when the number of luxurious articles in households increased. When the *raison d'etre* of the sampler had vanished, its popularity remained for it transformed itself into an ornamental picture acceptable to the age in which it found itself.

CHAPTER I

Early Samplers

IT is reasonable to suppose that samplers were fairly common in the Middle Ages though unfortunately no known example has survived. From evidence in hand, it is very likely that Anglo-Saxon women must have worked samplers in some form. The beauty and excellence of their needlework and their tapestries, in particular, were renowned on the Continent and the *Opus Anglicannum* was undoubtedly practised on some kind of sampler.

There is no *dated* sampler of Tudor work but Tudor samplers have been preserved. Figure 1 shows a specimen which is of particular interest on account of the fine execution of intricate cut and drawn work. The form assumes the arrangement of vertical bands of pattern work which was usual at the time. The details of the patterns include favourite motifs i.e. animal forms as represented by a crowned lion and a unicorn, lettering, geometrical flower patterns and S-forms.

The literature of the Tudor period makes ready reference to the custom of working samplers. Skelton, the poet laureate, in the reign of Henry VII refers in his writings to a " sampler to sow on ". Sir Philip Sidney in his "Arcadia" refers to a " beautiful sampler ". Turning the leaves of Shakespeare, one finds Helena addressing Hermia in "A Midsummer Night's Dream" :

> " O and is all forgot ?
> All schooldays' friendship, childhood innocence ?
> We, Hermia, like two artificial gods
> Have with our needles created both a flower
> Both on one sampler, sitting on one cushion
> Both working of one song, both in one key
> As if our hearts, our sides, our voices and our minds
> Had been incorporate."

In the well-known passage from " Titus Andronicus ", Marcus says,

> "Fair Philomel, she but lost her tongue
> And in a tedious sampler sew'd her mind."

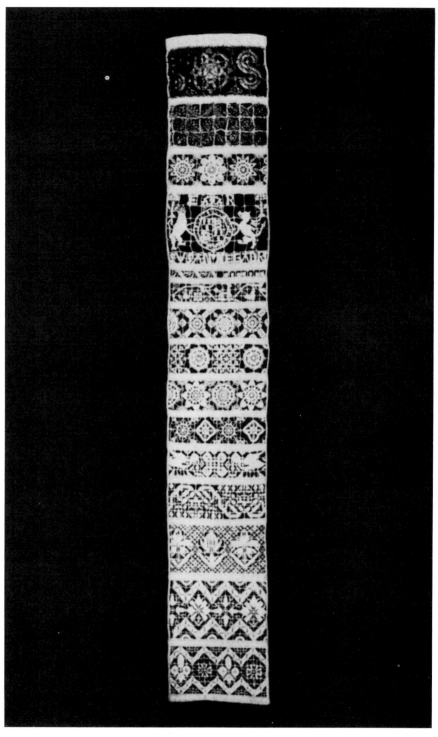

FIGURE 1.

Sampler of Tudor Needlework.

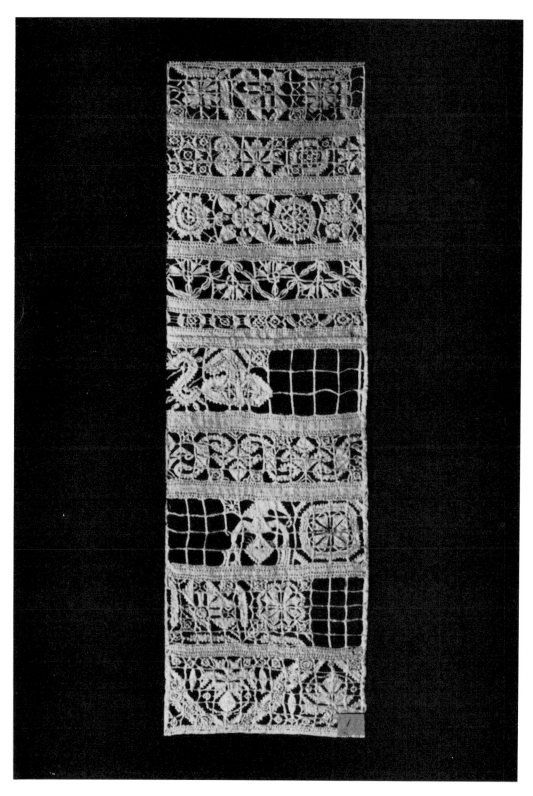

FIGURE 2.
Sampler in Linen with Cut and Drawn Work Panels.
Early 17th Century.

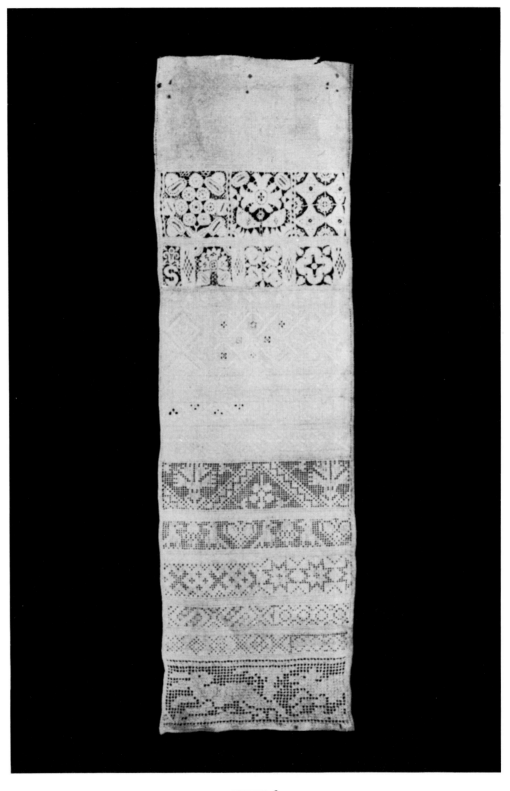

FIGURE 3.
Date 1650.   Size 27″ × 8″.   Drawn thread sampler,
natural linen worked in white.

FIGURE 4.
Sampler by Elizabeth Mackett in 1696

Shakespeare wrote in the reign of the Great Elizabeth but there is a particular reference to a sampler relating to the first Elizabeth of the Tudor dynasty. An inventory of 1502 records " an elne of linnyn cloth for a sampler for the Queen, viiJd."

A will proved at Boston on the 25th May, 1546, suggests that samplers were of intrinsic as well as of sentimental value. The will relates to a bequest by Margaret Thomson of Freston in Holland.

" I give to Alys Pynchebeck my syster daughter my sawmpler with semes."

On the death of Queen Elizabeth in 1601, one of her maids-of-honour worked " a sampler in red silk." The verse thereon became popular on samplers in subsequent generations, cataloguing as it did the virtues of the Great Queen. It was published later in a collection of " old Ballads " printed by J. Robs near Oxford Arms in Warwick Lane, 1725. It was entitled " A Short and Sweet Sonnet " and it was stated that it could be sung to the tune " Phillida Flouts Me ". The letters embroidered on the samplers ran :

> " Gone is *Elizabeth*
>> whom we have loved so dear.
> She our kind mistress was
>> full *Four* and *Forty* year
> *England* she governed well,
>> not to be blamed.
> *Flanders* she befriended
>> *Spain* she had toiled.
> *Papists* rejected
>> and the *Pope* spoiled.
> To *Princes* powerful
>> to the *World* vertuous.
> To her *Foes* merciful
>> To *Subjects* gracious.
> Her soul is in *Heaven*
>> the *World* keeps her glory.
> *Subjects* her good deeds
>> and so ends my *Story*.

Samplers were numerous in the 17th century and reference to them in the literature of the time are proportionately common. Among many writers, Herrick refers to samplers making special reference in

"Hesperides ". Thomas Milles writing in 1613 apparently condemns sampler-work for in his work " The Treasure of Auncient and Moderne Times ", he writes,

" Feare God and learne women's huswivery ;

Not idle Samplery or silken follies ; "

In contrast to this, William Hawkins in his "Apollo Shroving " written in 1627, advises

"Take out thy fescue and spell here in this one-learn'd booke,

Tell the stitches in this sampler of blacke and white."

The fescue was a pointer used in teaching children to read and the "Black and white " work refers to a colour harmony usual with both Elizabethan and Jacobean embroiderers which they used lavishly on samplers.

Milton in his " Comus " alludes to sampler work. There is an indication of a temporary loss of popularity of this form of needlework in the comment made by Dr. Johnson in the " Idler."

" Our girls forsake their samplers to teach kingdoms wisdom."

References to samplers can be traced in the writings of the 19th century writers ; but by the end of that age sampler-work had become well-established as part of the curriculum in a girls' school education and embroidering a sampler was henceforward taken for granted.

CHAPTER II

Utility and Ornament in Sampler Work

THE popularity of the sampler increased with the advance of the 17th century and continued unabated until towards the close of the 19th. By the samplers that they created more than anything else are we able to judge the skill of the women of those centuries in needlework.

During the early Stuart period, there was a marked development in the increase of luxury in personal clothing and domestic furnishings. As these articles increased in quantity as well as in quality, there was a greater demand for the marking and numbering of these. Moreover, many of the garments and articles embroidered were family heirlooms and identification marks were matters of pride as well as of utility. Ornamental alphabets and numerals embellished with many flourishes experienced a great vogue.

The extreme paucity of specimens prior to 1648 gives ballast to the opinion that on the downfall of the Stuart monarch, the Puritans made a holocaust of every sampler on which they could lay their hands. Moth and damp have, however, played a prominent part in the destruction of early specimens and it is fortunate that so many have been worked on coarse linen. Those worked in Victorian times on coarse loose canvas are apt to show signs of decay already while the older finer samplers have been enhanced and meliowed by Time. The clothing and furnishings for which the stitches and patterns were intended have perished but the samplers, not being subject to frequent use and, often-times being honoured as an exhibition of a young worker's skill, have escaped a destruction.

One of the earliest *dated* examples is the work of Rebeckah Pope and is preserved in the Victoria and Albert Museum. Dated 1644, it is made of cut work and appears to be part of a sampler rather than a completed one. It is left to the imagination to decide why the sampler is unfinished. Did the young worker tire of her task? Did she satisfy her instructress at an early stage as to her skill with her needle? Did Death or some misfortune cut short her labours? The sampler shows a row of cut and drawn work which is followed by another in coloured silks showing conventional rose trees, lilies and geometrical flower forms.

If the Puritans *did* destroy the existing samplers, they could not have been averse to the purpose of the samplers themselves. By the many specimens that have survived from the Puritan age, it is self-evident that these God-fearing men regarded the dexterious manipulation of the needle as a virtue among women, no doubt being inspired by the verses of Solomon wherein he epitomises his ideal woman:

" She seeketh wool and flax and worketh willingly with her hands.
She layeth her hands to the spindle and her hands hold the distaff
She maketh herself coverings of tapestry ;
                          her clothing is silk and purple."

Puritan mothers carried with them to America their skill with the needle and their inherited love of fine needlework. In the New World they established this tradition incorporating into it new and invigorating forces which they found existing there.

The reign of William and Mary saw a renaissance in household luxury. New ideas came to Britain from the Netherlands. Sampler-work was given a fresh impetus with the inrush of foreign patterns and motifs. The revived interest gathered strength in the reign of Queen Anne.

The Hanoverian dynasty also saw the introduction of new motifs and designs many of which reached Britain from the Continent. With the inrush of Methodism, the sampler deteriorated into a chart for texts and religious verses. Stitching and ornamentation were only of subsidiary interest. Samplers with texts and scripture pictures do not, however, belong exclusively to the age of Wesley. They had been in vogue in the 17th century. Jasper Mayne, writing in 1639, alludes to these in " The Citye Match ":

" Your school-mistresse . . . teaches
To knit in Chaldee *and worke Hebrewe samplers.*"

There have survived also from the 17th century examples of *knitted* samplers. Stitches and patterns are recorded, one young worker having worked an alphabet and a verse of poetry on a pair of mittens.

In the dame schools and in the later state schools, the sampler tended more and more to become an exercise in embroidery. From an aesthetic as well as from a utilitarian view-point the sampler at this stage underwent a slow process of disintegration. Design and colour harmonies were abandoned. The sampler appeared as an inharmonious conglomeration of figures and motifs, of letters and numerals, all huddled together within an elaborate ornamental border.

Individuality and attractiveness waned still further with the regimentation of the examination systems of the Board Schools where sampler work formed a soul searing task. Inspiration was inevitably lost when the needlework instructress had recourse to such tomes as Caulfields's " Dictionary of Needlework ", where, under the heading " To Make a Sampler " is found the instruction :

" Take some mosaic canvas of the first make and woven so that each thread is an equal distance apart. Cut this 18″ wide and 20″ long and measure off a border all round of 4 inches. For the border, half an inch from the edge, draw out threads in a pattern to the depth of half an inch and work over these with coloured silks. Then work a conventional scroll pattern in shades of several colours and in Tent stitch to fill up the remaining 3 inches of the border. Divide the sampler into three sections. In the top section work a figure design. In the centre an Alphabet in capital letters and in the bottom an appropriate verse, the name of the worker and the date."

The tragedy lies in the fact that these instructions were carried out with such exactitude !

Out-of-school samplers of the Victorian era are in keeping with the age. To modern eyes, they are over-ornamental, lacking in harmony of colour. Designs are crammed together to fill in a background as completely as is possible, the motifs having no unity (Figure 26) and the utilitarian aspect of the sampler fading out completely.

CHAPTER III

Foreign Sampler Work

COMPARED with other European countries, Britain appears to be the chief producer of samplers. Sampler work played an important part in the life of women on the continent and there was constant inter-play of ideas throughout the European countries concerning design and the embroidering of them.

Each country retained, at the same time, certain peculiar and traditional characteristics. The majority of Dutch samplers are short and square, suggesting a solidity of design and workmanship. Those of Britain, as will be seen, vary considerably in size and shape. Where Dutch designs were copied, they were executed with a lightness of touch and of colouring. Many of the motifs appearing on British samplers of the second half of the 17th century were imported from Holland. This was due to the influence of trade. There was a close personal link when members of the English royal family spent years of exile in the Netherlands and the bond was re-enforced when Dutch William of Orange became King of England. A favourite design was the heraldic arms of a city and darned samplers were much favoured in Holland.

Darned squares were also characteristic of German samplers with the peculiarity of having the material cut away from underneath. Like British samplers, those of Germany varied considerably in shape and in size and usually they were longer than they were broad.

The pattern books of Sibmacher printed in Nuremberg at the beginning of the 17th century emphasized geometric designs in particular. These were usually worked in black cotton and contemporary British samplers reflect this influence.

In comparison with the Dutch and the German, the French appear to have devoted less time to sampler work, judging by the number of specimens that have survived. Samplers were worked in the convent schools and a high standard of work was maintained. Many of the designs are religious in character for most of the needlework created had an ecclesiastical purpose. As with the Dutch and German samplers, pictorial designs are absent as are also texts and verses and records of the worker's age. The French excelled in emblems and floral designs in sprigs and borders. Sampler-workers of Britain copied these in order that they might be used on the elaborate apparel worn by men and women in the 18th and 19th centuries.

Italian influence on British samplers was strong particularly in the 16th and early 17th centuries when cut and lace work were so popular. Italian work was characterised by graceful coloured borders, coloured central work and geometrical designs of a floral type. The Venetian pattern books such as " Ostaus ", " La Vera Perffettione del Disegno", Parasole's " Pretiosa Gemma delle virtuose donne " and Vinciolo's " I singolari e nuovi Disegni ", published towards the latter half of the 16th century had a profound effect in popularizing geometrical designs suitable for cut and drawn work as shown on Figure 2, which is a British sampler worked in the early 17th century and shows cut and drawn white work in vertical panels on linen.

Scandinavian samplers were worked on muslin with intent of the construction of the designs and stitches later upon collars, elaborate fichus and similar neck and wrist wear. The ideas incorporated were adopted by Britain but in the nature of the case it is not possible to say exactly how far Scandinavian influence carried nor at what exact period.

Spanish and Mexican specimens of samplers are worked in coloured silks, often in bright colours. Drawn work is also shown and a considerable variety of stitches used. Cross-stitch is perhaps the most popular. Indeed so popular was it throughout the countries for this type of work that it was known as " sampler stitch ". The Mexican sampler shown on Figure 20 measures 17" × 18". It is worked in cross stitch on linen in bright greens, reds, yellows, fawns and blues. Lettering, conventional flower and bird forms are shown and also S-forms and trophies. Figure 19 is also a Mexican sampler being a square of 22". Here again patterns are in vertical bands. The work is on linen in bright colours of blue, red, green, fawn and yellow.

As in Britain, foreign samplers underwent a slow period of decay, dying naturally in that they had outlived their original purpose and also suffering acutely towards the end of their existence from a lack of originality. Earlier specimens therefore transcend later ones in beauty of workmanship and in design.

CHAPTER IV

The Work of Children

MOST of the British samplers have been worked by children. Some of the earlier samplers, judging by the high standard of the work and the skill evolved, must have been worked by adults. But sampler work was regarded traditionally as children's work. It was a common practice until comparatively recent times for every little girl to work her sampler.

From the mid-18th century, it became customary for children to endorse their sampler work with their names and ages. Earlier specimens though worked by children record no signatures nor ages. To-day, the main interest in these endorsements lies in the evidence of the remarkable skill shown by children of tender years. The absence of names and the intricate handwork on 16th century samplers suggest that they were more usually the work of adults. But there can be no fixed ruling on this, however. On some 17th century samplers a neatly worked verse seems to refute the theory emphasizing the fact the worker is an adult.

> When I was young I little thought
> That wit must be so dearly bought
> But now experience tells me how
> If I would thrive then I must bow
> And bend unto another's will
> That I might learn both art and skill
>
> To get my living with my hands
> That so I might be free from band
> And my own dame that I may be
> And free from all such slavery.
> Avoid vaine pastime fle youthfull pleasure
> Let moderation allways be thy measure
> And so prosed unto the heavenly treasure.

Militant feminism underlying this next verse suggest that this also was worked by an adult but in common with many elaborate verses of the

29

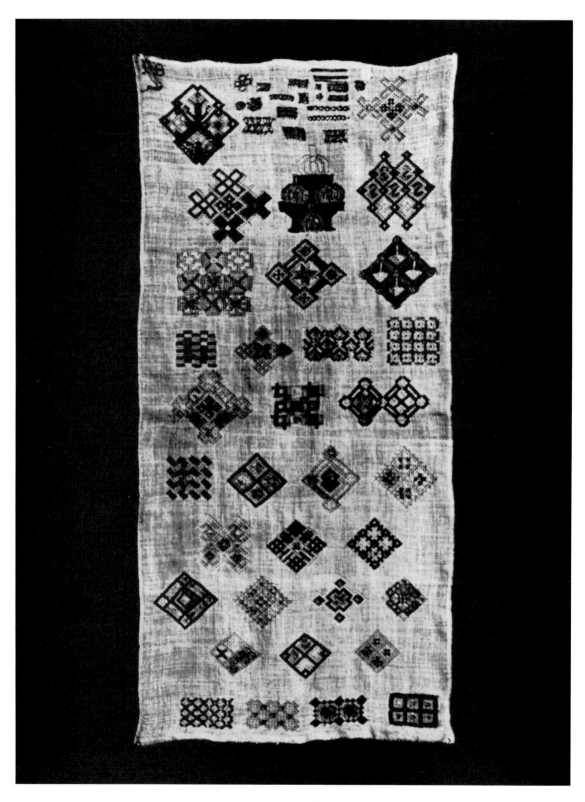

FIGURE 5.
Sampler showing stitches in coloured silks and metallic thread.

FIGURE 6.

George Morland Visit to the Boarding School.   Wallace Collection.

19th century, its philosophy may be entirely out of keeping with the age of the embroideress.

> Adam alone in Paradise did grieve
> And thought Eden a desert without Eve
> Until God pitying his lonesome state
> Crowned all his wishes with a lovely mate.
> Then why should man think mean or slight her
> That could not live in Paradise without her ?

A very usual design accompanying this verse was that showing Adam and Eve and the serpent on the Tree of the Knowledge of Good and Evil (See Figure 11). School samplers in particular were endorsed and bore the name of the charity school wherein they were worked (Figure 32). Signatures in different letterings and different settings are shown in Figures 13, 22, 27, 29. It must have been with pardonable pride that the young sempstresses worked in their names !

Until the advent of dame and state schools, girls received their instruction at home. It is very likely that a busy mother instructing her young brood would not be loath to include her young son in the sewing class were it primarily for her own peace of mind and satisfaction. Specimens do exist endorsed with a boy's name. More frequently a boy's name is included among a list of girl's names suggesting that a brother may have contributed to a family sampler. The colouring and lettering of such a signature are usually bolder than the others as more befitting to a masculine hand.

The motifs and stitches used on samplers were in such universal use that it is very difficult to determine where the samplers were worked. There does not appear to have been any local tradition of their working. The place where the sampler was worked is sometimes indicated after the signature. As has been shown this is very usual where the sampler was worked at a charity school Figure 32. The place is also sometimes suggested by a very usual verse which was embroidered on samplers ; though here again, it might be argued that a home town is indicated as the embroideress was at the time of working away from her home.

> Julia Cran is my name
> England is my nation
> Lichfield is my dwelling place
> And Christ is my salvation.

CHAPTER V

The Evolution of the Sampler

THE earliest samplers were real works of art (Figures 1 and 2). Often they were over a yard long. The one attributed to Elizabeth of York in the inventory was an ell in length, the English ell at that time being calculated at 45 inches. These early samplers were seldom over a quarter of a yard wide. This extreme narrowness is accounted for by the custom of rolling the sampler on a little ivory rod which was made for the purpose. The material used was a coarse linen which fortunately defies the onslaught of Time enabling these samplers to be examined in a perfect state of preservation. Deliberate order in the lay-out of the design does not characterise the earlier samplers as it does those of the latter half of the 17th century and those of the 18th century. That the earlier samplers emphasized utility rather than ornament is evident from the fact that many of the designs are shown in course of construction as well as in completed form. The primary purpose of the early samplers was to serve as an example of stitches and as an inspiration from which other patterns could be worked.

Work was usually done in vertical bands, some samplers containing as many as thirty different patterns of cut, drawn and lace work. This type of decoration was much in vogue in the 16th century as decoration for ruffs, collars and personal linen. The " punto in aria " work shown on samplers such as Figure 1 shows a high degree of proficiency which was maintained for a considerable period. Early specimens, for the greater part, were worked in white cotton and Figure 2 shows a sampler in linen with cut and drawn work in white stitches arranged in vertical panels. The bands are of varying widths. Lattice work is shown and a convential floral ornament including inter-lacing stems, geometrical patterns and the popular S-forms. Part of the cut and drawn work is filled with needle-point stitches. Flat satin stitch and eye-let holes shown on this sampler were usual on the early work. One combination of these stitches was known as " bird's eye pattern " or damask pattern. As an alternative to white work, floral and geometrical designs were sometimes worked in coloured silks.

Of these long banded samplers, many specimens are from three to

FIGURE 7.
17th century sampler worked on scrim showing use of metallic threads.

four feet in length, being only six to eight inches wide. Figure 3 is a sampler 27″ × 8″ and indicates the proportions usual in the samplers worked in vertical rows. This example is worked in white on natural linen and is dated 1650. Conventional geometric and floral patterns are shown and animal and bird forms are finely executed. Figure 4 shows the same type of work as done on the sampler of Elizabeth Mackett in 1696. Two rows of lettering are introduced and embroidery in coloured silks is shown on the upper section of the panel. Figure 5 shows a variation from working in strict vertical sections. The motifs are now separate entities placed over the background. The sampler was worked in the first half of the 17th century and shows stitches in coloured silks and also in metallic thread which was employed extensively in the " stump " work of the Jacobean period. The metal thread retained much popularity among sampler workers down to the close of the Victorian age. Where figures were introduced, it was worked so as to outline details of costume. The anatomy of insects, the veins of leaves, the wings of angels and of cupids were worked in metallic thread and coloured wax was introduced to represent buds of flowers. The metallic thread had a special fascination for sampler-workers who specialised in maps. Figure 7 shows a further use of metallic threads in conjunction with embroidery in coloured silks. The arrangement of pattern shows a further development away from confinement within horizontal bands and the work is done on scrim which on account of the loose weave of the threads, came to be very popular as a foundation with sampler workers.

The narrowness of the earlier samplers is partly explained · by the custom of rolling them when they were not in use but also by the narrowness of the material as it came from the hand looms. Moreover, the narrowness of the work was in keeping with the purpose of the sampler as an object for the practice and recording of patterns. A sampler of considerable length and of narrow breadth was a convenient one to handle. It was of sufficient width to gain proficiency and also to display the design. Further, by working in vertical bands, the sempstress was able to arrange several patterns on one sampler. Indeed it is as a collection of patterns rather than as objects of ornament that these banded samplers impress, beautiful as they are.

With the passage of time, the sampler was transformed from a pattern of stitches into a decorative ornament—usually of juvenile skill. Utility and ornament were, however, linked down to the close of the 17th century. In the following century, moral precept became of primary importance and the value of the sampler as a means whereby good needlework was acquired, diminished.

Although pride of place was given in the 18th century to long inscriptions, many patterns of the previous centuries were still copied extensively and new pictorial designs were introduced. Many of the samplers tended to copy the tapestry pictures which were so popular in Britain from the accession of William and Mary. Figures and houses, trees and birds appeared and these were often placed haphazardly on the linen. When inscriptions came to form the chief feature it was customary at first to work the lettering in black thread, which gave a funeral aspect to what was already a doleful verse. In complement to the inscription, the designs were worked in any spaces which were convenient on the background.

The samplers of the 18th century were worked for the greater part on linen. Scrim and later a canvas of fine wool became popular. The stitches most frequently used were cross stitch, long and short satin stitch, split and outline stitch. Coloured silks grew yet more popular and metallic thread brightened the work.

As it changed its function, the sampler changed its form. The long narrow panel was abandoned and the sampler became shorter and squarer. Narrow widths of material were still in use. A sampler might be worked in two pieces and the parts be joined together skilfully as in Figure 12. This sampler was worked between 1780 and 1800 and is signed Isabel Gray. The foundation is natural linen scrim and the stitches are worked in green and fawn, red and yellow. The upper section shows an alphabet with a floral band in vertical arrangement. The lower half has a modified vertical, symmetrical arrangement and shows trees, flowers, bird and crown motifs. Unity is given to the whole by the floral border of geometrical construction, which surrounds the whole.

An interesting earlier sampler showing two narrow panels joined is that shown on Figure 10. Its exact origin is unknown but the lettering declares it to be the work of Dorothy Greame and it is dated 1734. The whole measures 12″ × 8″ and the panels show vertical bands of lettering. The border between the two sections is elaborate and is worked in cross-stitch ; that at the sides of the sampler is simpler and uniform.

Borders grew in favour with the advance of the 18th century until they came to form an elaborate part of the decorative scheme. These borders were of several kinds. A usual form was a narrow wavy stem with small red, white and blue flowers as are shown in Figures 12 and 21. Sometimes the waving stem bore roses (Figures 14, 15 and 24), and pinks or very frequently strawberries (Figure 31). Narrow stripes, scrolls (Figure 18), and Greek fret pattern were much used as borders on account of the simplicity of working and of their effectiveness as part of the formal decoration. A flower and leaf arrangement (Figure 22) and triple leaf border (Figure 28), had many adherents. Figure 16 shows an elaborate border in cross stitch showing flower patterns in geometrical arrangement which forms a surround to an already elaborate figure picture.

Coarse unbleached canvas was used for samplers towards the close of the 18th century and its advent marks a distinct deterioration in design and stitchery. Cross-stitch, satin and eyelet stitches were worked in silks and wools, usually in red, green and blue. Pictorial motifs were crammed together (Figure 26). Rows upon rows of alphabets and numerals were separated by a zig-zag design or stripes. Small motifs were worked close to big ones and all available space was usually filled up with a conglomeration of figures, crowns, trees, dogs, hearts, stags, peacocks. Figure 25 is an example of this type. It was worked by Christine Maly, aged 7, and is dated 1834, showing that the absence of discriminate arrangement increased rather than diminished with the advance of the 19th century. The foundation of this sampler is linen scrim and it measures $16'' \times 12''$.

Occasionally, among 19th century specimens one comes across a sampler that deviates from the custom of creating a hotch-potch arrangement. Such are samplers which revive the old row upon row arrangement or work their patterns into horizontal sections or which succeed in spacing their designs in some pleasing manner. Elizabeth Barrett who worked a sampler $16'' \times 12''$ in 1824 (Figure 22), knew to a considerable degree the value of simplicity of arrangement. The motifs of her sampler are not displeasing in themselves nor in their placing. The lettering she worked in satin stitch and cross stitch in dark brown. The motifs and border are in green, brown and blue. Working a sampler five years earlier, MaryAnn Parke (Figure 21) had also completed a panel, which, compared with those customary at that period, is pleasing to modern eyes in its simplicity. Likewise the sampler of Gaenor Edwards, Figure 29, though more ambitious in its actual motifs achieves a distinctive simplicity in its arrangement.

From the middle of the 19th century, the sampler was much influenced by the wool work pictures worked in Berlin wool which were so popular with the Victorians. Brightly coloured wools were worked on coarse meshed canvas and the most usual designs were naturalistic flowers, landscapes and buildings. Towards the close of the century, architecture was much favoured on samplers. House designs were popular. Sometimes the little sempstress may have worked a design representing her own home (Figure 23), and notable buildings were also depicted.

CHAPTER VI

Colour Schemes

CAREFULLY chosen colour schemes are a distinctive feature of many samplers. A rise and fall in the standard of colour schemes is curiously concurrent with that of design. Black and white work was popular in the Elizabethan and Jacobean periods, reminiscent perhaps of the timbered architecture of the time. It marked an orientation towards colour work in that it led away from the white-work of the panels showing cut, drawn and lace work. The samplers of the Carolean period are characterised by a wonderful softness and delicacy. Delicate shades of pinks and greens and blues are blended harmoniously. The samplers worked in them are reminiscent of Japanese artistry at its best and the tones in the completed work suggest the delicate colourings of Liberty silks.

The abandonment of these colours and the consequent deterioration in colour harmonies which characterises sampler work executed towards the end of the 17th century followed on the introduction of a rough close textured canvas, yellowish-brown in colour. Bright colours were used with apparently the sole purpose of counter-acting its effect. But little thought was given to colour schemes in fashioning the motifs which were grouped closely together to eliminate the tones of the background.

A partiality to reds and greens marks the Georgian era. They are the prevailing colours in Figure 12. The sampler shown on Figure 28, shows that these colours were also much favoured in the Victorian age. The sampler, measuring 23" × 36" is the work of Hannah Johnson and is worked throughout in cross stitch in reds and greens. The reds worked on these samplers in common with others of the period are remarkable on account of their vividness. Due to the persistent nature of the dyes used, they retain even to-day after constant exposure to light their original shades of colouring.

On the whole, however, the majority of sampler workers in the 18th century paid but little attention to the effect of colouring. Most of the samplers are worked in dull shades, their prime interest being their long inscriptions. Colours are mixed together indiscriminately even within the formation of a single letter.

A very real, if unconscious effect on colouring was brought into the sampler work of the mid-18th century by the religious emphasis in the education of the young sampler workers. Sober and sombre colour schemes were sought to inscribe the moral precepts which now adorned samplers. Reds were abandoned almost entirely, the embroiderers confining themselves to the use of blues, yellows, blacks and greens. Blendings of these produced a quiet harmonious unity which was often satisfactory, especially when the sampler was not large. Victorian samplers often ran riot in colour as well as in design though at times samplers in which both these factors were satisfactory were created.

1 Sampler (1752) worked in silk thread on wool, mostly in satin and cross stitch.
Size 13 x 10 in. *(Victoria & Albert Museum)*

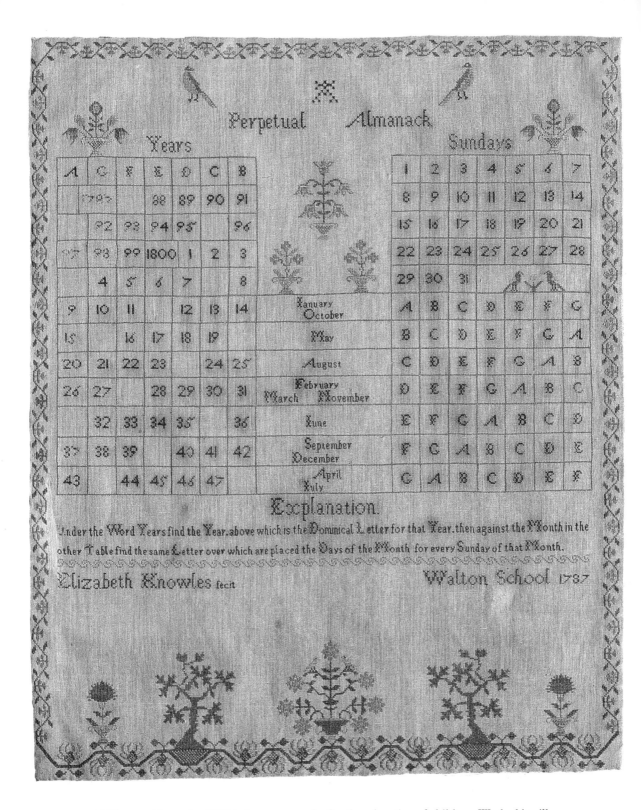

2 'Almanack' sampler (1787) of a type popular for the education of children. Worked in silk on linen. Size 16 x 13 in. *(Victoria & Albert Museum)*

3 Sampler (1834) embroidered on fine linen in cross stitch. Note the words, 'Miss Hughes's school' at the base. Size 23 x 21 in. *(Carmarthen Museum)*

As plants while tender bend which way you please
And are though crooked first made straight with ease
Yet if those plants to their full stature grow
Irregular they'll break as soon as bow
So youth set right at first with ease go on
And each new task is with new pleasure done
But if neglected till they grow in years
And each fond mother her dear darling spares
Error becomes habitual and we find
Tis then hard labour to reform the mind

A Representation of the National
School Newchurch

The above was work'd by Ann Stott Daughter of John and
Sarah Stott Sexton of St Nicholas Church Newchurch at the
Above school in the 13 year of her Age

4 Sampler embroidered in silk on linen scrim in cross stitch and satin stitch. The building depicted is evidently the worker's school. Mid nineteenth century (?). Size 23 x 24 in. *(Carmarthen Museum)*

CHAPTER VII

Stitches

THE stitches used in samplers were largely dependent on the patterns used. Geometrical patterns invited the use of satin stitch and it was also the most important of the stitches used in the early samplers showing white work. Needlepoint and eyelet stitches were also used extensively in the early samplers.

Towards the middle of the 17th century trellis stitch acquired favour. It appears also on the earliest known English samplers. It was popular partly on account of its being a stitch easy to execute and on account of its unusual attractiveness.

Darning stitch became popular particularly when wool was used (Figures 8 and 9). Attractive results were obtained by using it in the form of needle-weaving.

Hollie stitch was another favourite as it lent itself so admirably to coloured work. It was used especially for delicate effects such as the centres of petals and calices of flowers.

Marking cross stitch was another favourite. It was perhaps the most popular of all stitches and was used so much that it came to be known as "sampler stitch". The more usual form was to work it so that a neat square was built up at the back. As an alternative, the stitch was sometimes worked so that the square appeared uppermost and the cross underneath.

FIGURE 8.
Sampler Size 14″×5″. Worked by Rebecca Crompton, London. Needleweaving in natural linen worked in horizontal bands.

FIGURE 9.
Sampler of pattern darning worked by Rebecca Crompton, London. Size 4″ × 18″. Worked in horizontal bands of straight stitches on natural canvas, in various bright colours.

CHAPTER VIII

Pattern Books

MANY of the patterns on samplers were copied by one generation from another. Apart from this form by tradition, there existed a literature on the subject which dates from the 16th century. Pattern books on lace-work were very plentiful both in Britain and on the continent but sampler pattern books were fewer in number.

The earliest pattern book which has survived was produced in 1591. It is significant that it was a translation from an Italian work. Italy has always excelled in fine cut work and this was a form of needlework which experienced a great vogue in the 16th century. The title of the earliest known sampler pattern book is no more elaborate than the designs within, *"New and Singular Patternes and Workes on Linnen Serving for Patternes to make all Sortes of Lace Edgngs and Cut Workes : Newly invented for the Profite and Contentment of Ladies and Gentilwomen and others that are desirous of this Art. By Vincentio. Printed by John Wolfe 1591."*

Books published in the Elizabethan period were embellished with wood-cuts and these were often copied by embroiderers. The out-standing books of needlework of the 17th century are Shoreleyker's " Schole-house for the Needle " 1624 and the more familiar work, " The Needle's Excellency ". By 1640 the latter work had run into twelve editions. A well-used but very interesting copy of it is preserved in the British Museum. Its full title rivals that of Vincentio's pattern book of 1591 being " *A Booke wherein are divers admirable workes wrought with the needle. Newly invented and cut in copper for the pleasure and profite of the industrious.* Printed by John Boler and are to be sold at the Syne of the Marigold in Paules Churchyard." This book makes no direct mention of sampler work but its use for that purpose may be inferred from the reference to articles for which samplers would be required " to wit hand-kerchiefs, table cloaths for parlours or for halls, sheetes, towels, napkins, pillow beares." Prefixed to the book is a poem by a well–established poet, John Taylor, wherein he states :

" Herein practise and invention may be free
And as a squirrel skips from tree to tree
So maids may (from their mistresse or their mother)
Learne to leave one worke and to learne another.
For here they may make much choice of which is which
And skip from worke to worke, from stitch to stitch
Until, in time, delighful practise shall
(With profite) make them perfect in them all.
Thus hoping, that these workes may have their guide
To serve for ornament and not for pride :
To cherish virtue, banish idlenesse
For these ends may this book have good successe."

In these lines does John Taylor catalogue the purpose of sampler working and in the following lines he indicates the nature of the designs shown in the book.

" Flowers, Plants and Fishes
Beasts, Birds, Flyes and Bees
Hills, Dales, Plains and Pastures
Skies, Seas, Rivers, Trees.
There's nothing ne'er at hand or farthest sought.
But with the needle may be shap'd and wrought."

In later days there must have been many illustrations of lettering and ornamentation for the guidance of the young in sampler making. Many of these were in all likelihood not bound in book form and this would account for the ephemeral nature of their existence. But few traces of them now remain.

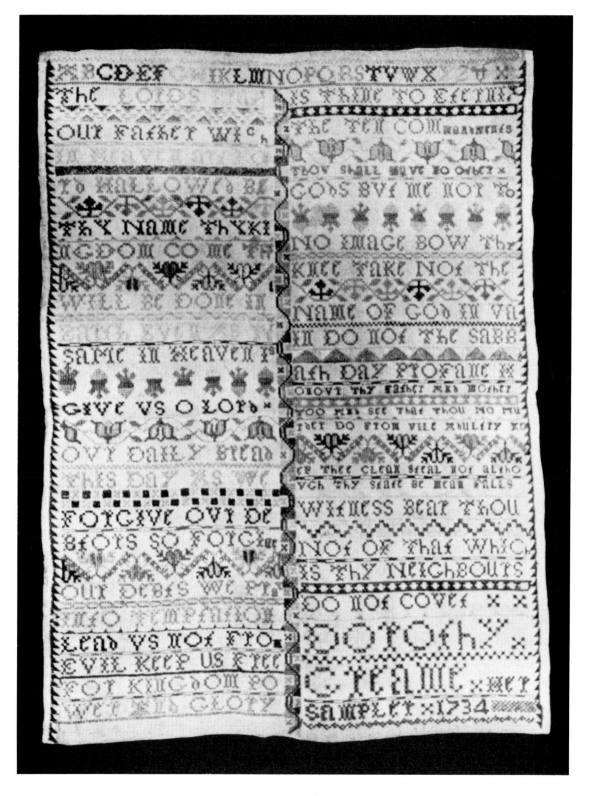

FIGURE 10.
Origin Unknown. Dorothy Greame dated 1734. Worked in two vertical bands of lettering.
Size   12″×8″

FIGURE 11.

Date 1760. Size 3″ × 15″, 4″ × 5″. Housewife and case. Design worked in cross stitch on linen bound with pink; motifs include Adam and Eve, angels, ship, birds, animals and flowers.

FIGURE 12.
Approximate date 1780-1800. Signed Isabel Gray. Worked in green, fawn, red, and yellow on natural linen scrim. Worked in two parts surrounded by floral border. Upper section shows alphabet and floral bands; the lower trees, flower and bird motifs with crowns.

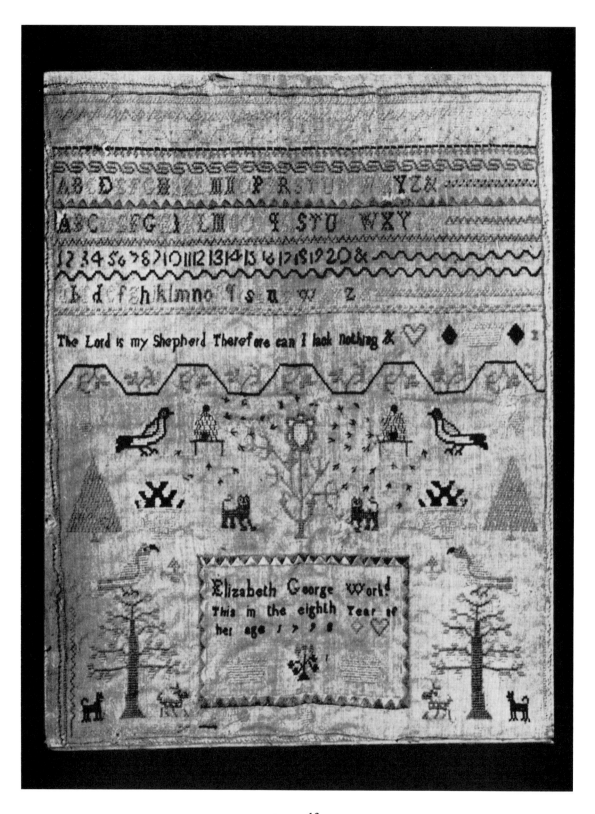

FIGURE 13.
British Sampler dated 1790. Signed Elizabeth George. Worked in greys, green, brown with design of birds, trees and alphabets.

CHAPTER IX

School Samplers

SAMPLERS were very usual in the dame and early state schools. Many quaint samplers were worked in them at a tender age. In Wheatley's picture of " The Schoolmistress " (frontispiece) which was engraved in stipples by Coles in 1794 the sampler as a form of instruction is emphasized and it would appear that design, by tradition rather than from the inspiration of a pattern book, was the more usual in places of instruction. In the picture a small child is embroidering a sampler and among those waiting the attention of the old dame is an older girl. She is holding a sampler on which a complete alphabet appears to have been worked. The picture by George Morland in the Wallace Collection entitled "Visit to the Boarding School ", Figure 6, also indicates that the working of a sampler was an important task.

It has been suggested that through the sampler a young child learnt the alphabet. Familiarity with the letters themselves and their sequence must have been fostered by the sight of them on samplers. The sampler must have been primarily, however, a lesson in *needlework*.

The working of samplers could not have been particularly popular with the young people who made them. The embroidering of maps for instance could not have afforded much relief from the dry matter-of-factness of the geography lesson of earlier times with their long recitatives of place names of countries, inlets, counties and towns, nor was the embroidering of moral precept an attractive form of relaxation from the study of the scriptures. The samplers must in many cases represent a task that must be endured perforce by the young child. Ambitious parents, however, as well as self-satisfied instructors must have regarded the embroidered panels with considerable affection—an affection which resulted in the preservation of many of them as they were relegated to the place of being family heirlooms.

51

The sampler must have played a prominent part in Charity Schools (Figure 32),for they served as testimonials of the standard of work executed. Figure 30 is an interesting specimen.   It may have been that the sampler was a medium of teaching the Welsh language or alternatively the two texts worked by Gaenor Edwards at Oswestry represent an effort to preserve the language in the Border Country.

Utility as well as ornament may have characterised sampler work of charity schools in especial.   Articles such as the housewife, shown on Figure 11 would be most likely to appeal to the patrons and the instructors.

FIGURE 14.

Square Sampler Size 12″ × 12″. Dated 1797. Signed Mary Ann Chambers. Verse "Spring" worked in browns and greens in cross, satin and star stitch.

FIGURE 15.

Sampler probably of Georgian period showing alphabets, numerals, conventional motifs and male and female figures.

FIGURE 16.

Embroidered Picture, the work of Mary Man.   Sampler-type border.

FIGURE 17.
Size 11″ × 6″.   Embroidery in green, blue and orange on natural linen.

FIGURE 18.

Size 11″ × 12″. Signed Kattay Allan. Worked in bands of flowers and letters in red and green on cream.

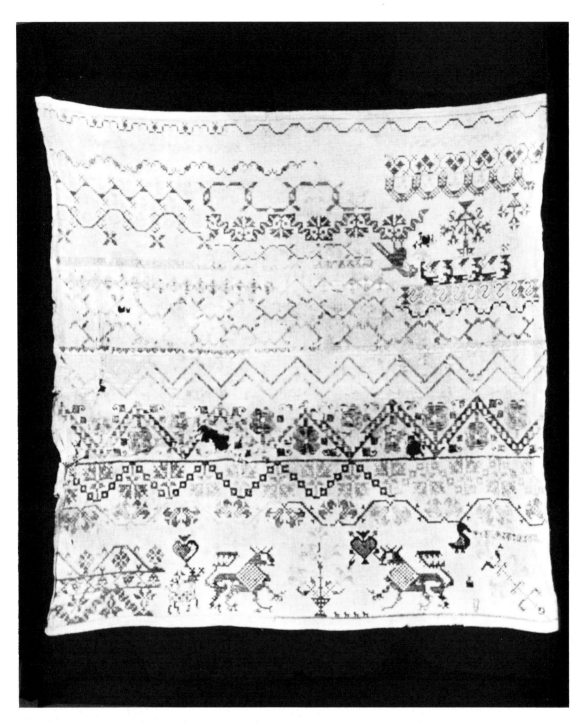

FIGURE 19.
Mexico; Size 22″ × 22″. Worked in bands of blue, red, green, fawn and yellow on linen.

FIGURE 20.

Mexico; Size 17″ × 18″. Cross stitch worked on linen in greens, blues, fawns, reds and yellows.

FIGURE 21.

Size 26″ × 8″. Dated 1819. Signed Mary Ann Park. Worked on linen scrim.

CHAPTER X

Details of Design and Ornament

THE earlier samplers possess decorative patterns of a high standard. Many of the actual designs in later specimens are good but their value is lost through the massing of many subjects on to one canvas. Many of the designs used were favoured by contemporary workers on the continent so that there was a kind of European standardization of ornament. In " The Needle's Excellency," John Taylor makes far-reaching claims for the sources of the patterns shown in that book,

" From the remotest part of *Christendome*
Collected with much paines and industrie,
From scorching *Spaine* and freezing *Muscovie*
From fertill *France* and pleasant *Italy*,
From *Poland, Sweden, Denmark, Germany*
And some of these rare patternes have beene fet
Beyond the bounds of faithlesse *Mahomet*
From spacious *China* and those Kindoms East
And from great *Mexico*, the *Indies* West."

The European source of these world-wide sampler designs was, however, Italy. Italian pattern books were in high favour and their translation into English, French and German resulted in a certain ubiquitousness of sampler motifs. Most sampler workers were content with copying patterns which had received universal approval but samplers exist which are refreshing in their originality. The young embroiderer might try to illustrate her garden, her pet or her home. Ann Hibbert whose sampler is shown in Figure 23, may have accomplished this object as may also have the more ambitious Gaenor Edwards (Figure 29) who worked her sampler of cross stitch in 1843. Thatched cottages were frequently delineated ; Georgian houses were worked, being favoured perhaps because they were easy to work. On the whole, originality was frowned upon for patterns once accepted were copied by each generation in a family. On account of this custom of copying, it is very difficult to

61

attempt to date a sampler which has not been endorsed with the year of its completion.   Love of architecture characterised the Victorians and they delineated buildings with remarkable exactitude.   A sampler showing a thatched cottage or some other picturesque construction cannot, however, be attributed to the 19th century on that account for samplers worked in the Stuart period show motifs of this kind set against naturalistic backgrounds.

When introducing such designs, the originators failed to understand that the pictorial is not suitable for reproduction in embroidery.   In equal measure, they over-looked the fact that the delineation of the human figure is never successful in embroidery unless treated as decorative only.   The sampler workers made the mistake of trying to reproduce them realistically e.g. Figure 30.

This introduction of *human figures* into sampler embroidery is a natural development for they were very usual in tapestries and in many forms of needlework since the Renaissance.   Coloured silks were used most frequently to depict costume, the details thereof being worked in metallic thread.   In this the embroiderers copied the stump work of the 17th century but the sampler workers did not seek a raised effect.

The figures that appear on samplers are peculiar.   They are often small and stiff with their arms extended.   Even when they adopt another attitude, there remains the common denominator of a close-fitting costume. The figures in the earlier specimens were sometimes known as " Boxers " because of the aggressive attitude suggested by the extended arms.   By the middle of the 18th century, the figures had changed their attitude. They were now shown bearing a trophy in one hand.   Opinion is divided as to the nature of this trophy, some regarding it as a symbol of aggressiveness, others as a peace token deliberately negativing pugnacity.   Later, the trophy was shown as a garland or a crown.   Some endeavour to trace the pedigree of this emblem whatever it was meant to imply, by way of the cupids of the Renaissance and the Amores of the Romans to the Erotes of the Greeks.

Nor is the modern connoisseur alone perplexed by the nature of the trophy. The Victorian sampler worker seems to have been often perplexed as to its exact structure.   It is sometimes shown in the form of a conventional cup trophy which became in itself a very usual motif (Figures 12 and 24).   Sometimes it is shown as a spray with branches or leaves on either side.   It is sometimes a four-petalled flower.   Often it is in the form of an acorn, a favourite subject of design in the Stuart period.   More ambitious workers converted the trophy into an intricate candleabra.   This form also developed as a separate unit and was at times particularly attractive. Linked with a tree formation it was used by Martha Lungley Danbury on the top and bottom sections of her sampler as shown in Figure 27.

The little figures themselves are dressed much alike throughout the ages. The costumes are close-fitting. Men's clothes comprise a tight-fitting coat and knee breeches. Women's clothes also fit close to the figure and they often don snow-white aprons with voluminous strings. In many instances the young embroiderer may have portrayed the costume prevailing in her day. Such was perhaps the case in Figures 15 and 30. A sarcastic-humorous note is introduced at times when a human figure is shown with the appertunances of the devil. Tradition maintains that the God-fearing Oliver Cromwell was so portrayed on the samplers of Royalist children! Georgian costume is often shown. The efforts in creating these human figures were painstaking enough but the total effect, to modern eyes, is disappointing for they fit but uncomfortably into the scheme of decoration. A realistic effect was often sought but the sampler worker or those instructing her, failed to understand that the lights and shades of painting could not be introduced through the flat medium of canvas and cross stitch.

Symbolic figures were worked as well as human figures. The Creator, the Virgin Mary, Christ, the apostles and angels were worked and also figures representing Mercy, Justice, Vengeance and such like. With the advent of Methodism, Bible stories were illustrated. Figure 16 shows an elaborate and quaint rendering of the sacrifice of Isaac. It is worked in various colours and stitches. It has on it the name "Mary Man" but records no age, date or place. Surrounding it is an elaborate border of cross-stitch in the type of design usual in sampler work. The cherub-messenger shown in the left-hand corner was much in favour with child workers. A more attractive example of it appears on Figure 31. Adam and Eve under the Tree of Knowledge (Figure 11), the finding of Moses, Elijah being fed by the ravens and the flight into Egypt were usual themes. Another usual subject was the marriage of Herod, showing Salome with the head of John the Baptist. Strictly speaking, these are embroidered pictures not sampler-work proper and represent a stage in advance of that in which the young sempstress practised her needle on a sampler.

A human figure is sometimes worked in personal affection. A specimen preserved in the Victoria and Albert Museum and dating from the first half of the 19th century shows a sampler in woollen canvas worked in coloured silks. Among the conventional trees, animals and birds worked thereon is shown a small square house. At the bottom of the rectangle stands the figure of a soldier or pensioner wearing a red long-tailed coat, dark breeches and a cocked hat. Above is the inscription " This is my dear Father ".

Tapestry workers had favoured *animal forms* but sampler workers at first seem to have made an effort to boycott their inclusion for they did not lend themselves readily to a narrow vertical row arrangement. Stags and unicorns had been popular on tapestries, the former holding precedence. The order was reversed on samplers. The lion, leopard, stag, ox and rabbit were very usual. The stag seems to have been neglected until the middle of the 18th century but once it had established itself it appeared very frequently. In an elaborate form it is embroidered on the housewife shown in Figure 11. Elizabeth George who completed her sampler in 1798 worked a stag at the foot of her work (Figure 13). The recumbent stags at the foot of her sampler must have gladdened the heart of eleven-year-old Margaret Crighton as she stitched away at the Free School of St. Paul's at Edinburgh in 1853 (Figure 32).

The lion was often worked on samplers. Its form is varied. Sometimes it appears as a unicorn. It is also shown as the wearer of the crown, this possibly being symbolic of Britain's might (Figure 14). The sampler shown at Figure 28 was completed by Hannah Johnson when 18 years of age. It has a border of animals and birds worked in solid cross stitch. The dog shown on Figure 29 may be an attempt at faithful reproduction.

On the whole, the animal forms depicted are not successful. This is due to the fact that, as with human figures, the finished work had in it a semblance of caricature due to an effort to depict realistically in an unsuitable medium.

Bird forms lend themselves more graciously to needlework and appear in different representations on many samplers (e.g. Figures 11, 13, 14, 26, 29). The eagle was shown on early samplers and the peacock with its tail lending itself to elaborate decoration was frequently shown on later ones (Figure 24).

The samplers created in early Stuart times show insects such as caterpillars, snails and flies. These motifs had been usual in " stump " work. Moreover, they had formed a feature of decorative art as early as the 15th century when monastic artists had used them for the illumination of manuscripts. Adaptations of these were often seen on samplers (Figure 27).

Flowers lend themselves favourably to embroidery. They were much used by sampler workers on account of their great variety of form. Possibly too, there existed a well-developed love of flowers in the hearts of the young workers of unindustrialised Britain. Some flower motifs were more popular than others on account of their being national badges. Many of the flowers portrayed were those which grew in the ornamental gardens of the Britain of the 17th and 18th centuries and in many instances may have been modelled from living specimens. Linked with flower motifs were leaves of trees (Figure 17), those of the oak and yew being popular as was also the vine. Of flower heads, the marigold and the clover were much used but the prime favourite was the rose. (Figures 21 and 28).

The rose had a national significance in Britain, being the emblem of both the Lancastrian and Yorkist parties in the Wars of the Roses prior to their blending in the attractive Tudor Rose. This rose was familiar to sampler workers on account of its prominence on the insignia of the realm and as it was engraved on the national coinage. Its most usual form on a sampler is as a full-blown rose which is single not double. Most frequently it was worked in red or in white ; sometimes in a combination of both. A development of the motif is shown in the embroidering of a whole rose-bush as in Figure 25 or the flowers were placed in a rose-bowl (Figure 26), which in itself perpetuated the trophy of the old-time " Boxers ". The rose was also shown in profile or in bud, some of the latter being represented by touches of wax. Foreign samplers emphasized the decorative value of the rose and this fact added to its prestige, increasing its popularity in embroidery in this country.

The carnation or pink had established itself in early times as a motif in needlework. The tapestry workers of Persia had made good use of it, recognizing its decorative value. Sampler-workers up to the close of the 17th century appear to have been even more partial to it than to the rose. Figure 7 shows it embroidered in conjunction with the use of metallic threads. Figure 12, shows variation of it as part of the decorative scheme. In Figure 26 its prime purpose seems to be to fill in the background.

Trailing plants were useful botanical specimens to copy on account of their adaptability to several uses. The vine and the honeysuckle were much favoured. Climbing plants, botanically unidentifiable, often served as borders. (Figures 21 and 22).

The strawberry is believed to have been introduced into Britain at the end of the reign of Queen Elizabeth. It became a favourite motif in Jacobean embroidery for the workers of that period loved motifs which had quick, bold effects. Both the flower and the fruit were copied on samplers, particularly in the first half of the 17th century. When its first popularity had passed away, it regained favour as a border pattern, the later examples being faithful copies of the borders which had been created a century earlier. Figure 26 and Figure 31 show usual versions of it.

Both the floral and the vegetable kingdoms offered a wide selection to the sampler-worker. Certain motifs however succeeded in establishing themselves early and workers from one generation to another clung tenaciously and conservatively to them. Embroidered tulips suggest the influence of Dutch samplers. Thistles may perhaps represent the work of Scottish embroiderers. The oak, oak leaf and acorn (See Figure 17), enjoyed a vigorous popularity partly, as has been said because of the events connected with the flight of Charles I. The leaves were often worked in rows and were sometimes made to form a border. The flower motifs of the earlier samplers show a blending of realistic representation and geometrical form.

The Victorians paid very deliberate attention to architecture and this trend showed itself even in the depicting of buildings upon samplers. The structures are at times surprisingly realistic and detail is most minute. (Figures 29 and 30). But the majority of embroiderers, being affected by the Berlin wool-work patterns contented themselves with producing romantic, impossible buildings surrounded by naturalistic landscapes. Formal little houses of Georgian pattern retained considerable favour (Figure 28), and there was a decided partiality for oriental temples (Figure 28). The Berlin wool-workers reproduced buildings of national importance such as those of well-known cathedrals, Henry VIII's royal palace of Nonsuch; or inspiration came from the Bible and the Tower of Babel or Solomon's Temple were portrayed. Penrhyn Castle worked on the sampler shown on Figure 30 is an example of how the sampler-workers adapted the patterns of the wool workers for their own use.

At the end of the 17th century a *crown* or a *coronet* became a very usual motif. A coronet placed over the initials or name of the worker is regarded by some as evidence that the sampler-worker was a lady of title. Placed over a series of initials it may have suggested the names of patrons (Figures 18 and 32). Crowns were very usual on continental samplers and a fresh impetus was given to their use in Britain with the flood of foreign motifs that flowed into the country with the accession of William and Mary. The establishment of the House of Hanover increased rather than stemmed the flow. It was sometimes worked in outline (Figure 32), and sometimes formed an elaborate motif (Figure 29).

Not only did the crown or coronet lend itself to varied construction, the whole feudal hierarchy being emblazoned at times upon one sampler, but it was in itself a useful motif. Assembled together, crowns served as useful borders. Worked in rows they filled up spaces and they were useful in completing a line not filled in with lettering (Figure 10).

Hearts appear on British specimens (Figure 26), but with far less frequency than they do on foreign specimens (Figure 19). Fruits were also worked, a form resembling the pineapple being an intricate motif sometimes favoured.

Borders. The earliest samplers were worked in rows and had no kind of decorative frame-work. A surround or border for the whole was first evolved by making use of one of the rows in the sampler as an edging. The advantage and decorative value of a border was soon seized upon and but few of the later specimens appear without one. Borders became very usual at the beginning of the second quarter of the 18th century and their appearance synchronizes with the change of the sampler to a squarer form. Stripes and Greek fret pattern were much used for early borders as were also scroll forms (Figure 18). The advantages of a trailing stem which could be made to bear all manner of flowers and which could at need be made to adopt a stiff angular form was realised. Figures 11, 16, 22 and 23, show borders varying in design and elaboration.

Alphabets and numerals were absent from the earliest samplers. They were filled with decorative designs only. Lettering and numbering became essential in Stuart households and children were taught the art by the manipulation of the needle. Alphabets in capitals and small letters were worked in rows and these were copied very accurately by children a century later (Figures 13 and 31). In the 18th century, lettering was created which was over-elaborate to the point of being florid. Some Victorian samplers show alphabets in rows separated by elaborate borders but the tendency towards the end of that age was to omit them entirely from the sampler.

Some of the early samplers retain a personal note in that they bear the initials of the worker. Partly as an exercise in lettering and partly as a testimonial of skill, signatures came to be worked in full. A child worker would proudly inscribe her work with an inscription such as " Christina Goolden her Work in the Tenth Year of her Age, MDCCXCVI ". It became customary in the latter half of the 18th century for a child to enter her age as well as her name. There is pathos as well as admiration in the fact that most of the young sampler workers needed only one figure to represent their age ! The lettering exercise might in many cases have served as a lesson in orthography.

Ann Hunt who worked an elaborate sampler in 1770, bearing many motifs symmetrically arranged and a border with a hunting scene was befogged in the spelling of her inscription.

> " Friends are like leaves that on trees
>   do grow : in summer's prosp'rous state
>   much Love the show.   but art thou in
>   adversity than they. like laves from
>   trees in autum fall away."

She adds :

> " this
> work in ha
> nd my friends
> mey have whe
> n.   I am dead and
> laid in grave."

Among several quaint specimens of this type is one in which the embroideress records " with my nedel I rout the same." The place where the work was done is sometimes entered, especially when it served as an exercise in a charity school (Figure 32).

It is to be regretted that the value of the sampler as a social document is so small. Samplers reflect all too little the historical background of the worker. But rarely is a national or historical event recorded.

Two samplers which make historical reference are preserved in the Ellis Collection at the Maidstone Museum. One commemorates William of Orange and Queen Mary and another records the sympathy prevalent in Britain on the death of Queen Caroline. One feels that one could sacrifice willingly masses of peacocks, temples, coronets, garlands, alphabets and numerals for inscriptions such as these.

> " The Prince of Orange landed in the West of England on the 5th November, 1688, and on the 11th of April, 1689, was crowned King of England and in the year 1692 the French came to invade England and a fleet of ships sent by King William drove them from the English seas and took singed and burned 21 of their ships.

> Martha Wright, March 26, 1693."

FIGURE 22.

British 1824.   Size 16″ × 12″.   Signed Elizabeth Barrett.   Verse worked in satin stitch and cross stitch in dark brown.   Border in green, brown and blue.

FIGURE 23

Sampler worked by Mary Ann Hibbert 1825.

FIGURE 24.

Size 18″×16″.   Signed Isabella Blackburn aged 9.   Worked in natural scrim in cross stitch in green, red, yellow, purple and blue.

FIGURE 25.
Signed Christine Maly aged 7.   Worked in linen scrim.   Date 1834.   Size 16″ × 12″.

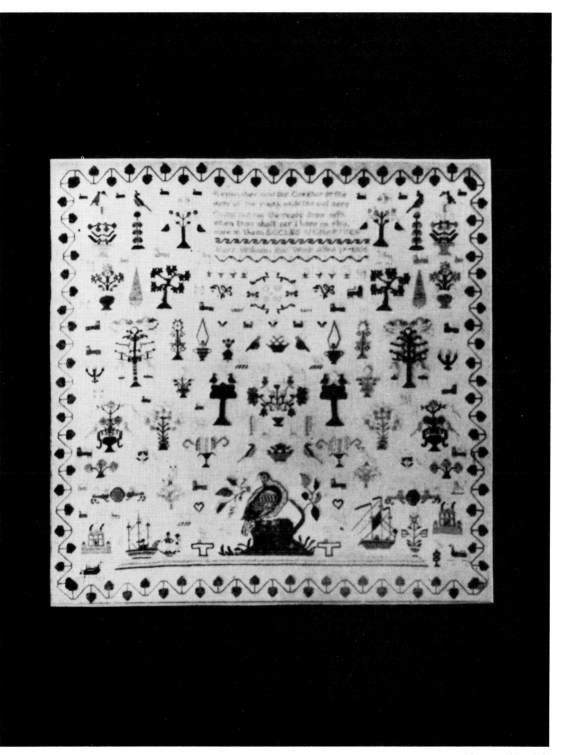

FIGURE 26
Sampler by Mary Williams, 1835.

Jesus permit thy Gracious name to Stand
The first effort of an Infant hand .
And whilst her Fingers on the canvas move
Engage her tender heart to seek thy love
With thy dear children let her have her part .
And write these words thyself upon her heart
Martha . Lungley . Danbury . 1836 ___

FIGURE 27.
British sampler. Dated 1836. Size 17″ × 12″. Signed Martha Lungley Danbury. Verse in dark brown with band of trees above, and birds and houses below. Green floral border in cross and chain stitch on natural linen.

Had many sampler workers recorded events of local or of national interest as did Mary Minshull in the following inscription, considerable material of social interest would have been preserved for posterity.

"There was an earthquake on the 8th September, 1692, in the city of London but no hurt tho' it caused most part of England to tremble."

A sampler commemorating the Peace of Amiens 1802 bears the inscription :

"Past is the storm and o'er the azure sky serenely shines the sun
With every breeze the waving branches nod their kind assent."

In 1829 Elizabeth Jane Gates worked a sampler which reflects the feelings of those agitating for the abolition of slavery which was put into effect four years later :

"THERE'S mercy in each ray of light, that mortal eye e'er saw.
THERE'S mercy in each breath of air, that mortal lips can draw
THERE'S mercy in each bird and beast, in God's indulgent plan.
THERE'S mercy for each creeping thing—But Man has none for Man."

CHAPTER XI

Inscriptions

THE inscriptions worked upon samplers are a literature in themselves. These more than any other feature, give clues to the social back-ground of the young sampler-workers.

Alphabets and numerals grew too monotonous in working despite the introduction of florid lettering. The signature of the worker and the embroidering of the year in which it was worked allowed insufficient scope for children grown skilful with the needle. In the 18th century it became customary to inscribe an old saw upon a sampler. Later Bible texts were worked such as " Remember now thy Creator in the days of thy youth." Rhymes were also worked, these being at first embroidered continuously as prose. As the century advanced it became fashionable to embroider long moral inscriptions and religious verse.

A very usual verse which marks the transition from saws to religious inscription and which was copied extensively in later years was that taken from Proverbs which states :

" Favour is deceitful
And Beauty is Vain
But a Woman that feareth the Lord
She shall be praised."

The Lord's Prayer, the Ten Commandments and the Apostles' Creed were often inscribed upon samplers, the embroideress seeking inspiration for her lettering from the elaborate scrolls painted on the walls of churches which were frequently adorned with these Biblical passages. Full-length figures from Biblical history sometimes adorned such samplers or the worker would content herself with the introduction of robust cherubs. Specimens exist where a French or Hebrew version of the scriptures has been worked alongside the English or instead of it. This testifies less to proficiency of the sempstress as a linguist than to her ability at copying the illuminated pages which lent colour and charm to family bibles.

The prevalence of religious verses is accounted for by the surge of Methodism which spread through Britain in the 18th century. Religious

77

books formed the bulk of children's reading at that time and many of the verses are taken from them. The main sources of the inscriptions were " *Divine and Moral Songs for Children* " by Isaac Watts, 1720, the hymns of the Wesleys and the hymns of Dr. Dodderige. The themes of the verses are usually doleful, the vanity and futility of youth is emphasized and passionate longing for Heaven is recorded.

Religious festivals were commemorated on samplers. Easter was celebrated by many verses, the two most usual being,

> " See how the lilies flourish white and fair
> See how the ravens fed from heaven are ;
> Never distrust thy God for cloth and bread
> While lilies flourish and the Raven's fed."

and

> " The holy Feast of Easter was enjoined
> To bring Christ's resurrection to our mind
> Rise then from sin as he did from the Grave
> That by his Merits, he your souls may save."

Akin to festival religious verses were inscriptions to the seasons such as that eulogising Spring on Figure 14, Christmas was often hailed with the short inscription " Glory to God in the Highest ". The Crucifixion was a very usual form on samplers worked on the continent but it is but seldom portrayed on those of Britain.

Many inscriptions dedicate the work to Christ. Some commemorate a patron. The verse on Figure 27 was frequently copied. Prayers for use at morning and at evening were embroidered, an example of one of these being shown on Figure 14. Some reference to the teacher or benefactor was often introduced into the samplers worked at charity schools. No inference of sarcasm was intended in such verses as :

> " Oh smile on those whose liberal care
> Provides for our instruction here ;
> And let our conduct ever prove
> We're grateful for their generous love."

There is unconscious humour in the mixing of metaphors and sentiments :

> " Oh may thy powerful word
> Inspire a breathing worm
> To rush into thy Kingdom, Lord,
> And take it as by storm.

> Oh may we all improve
> Thy grace already given
> To seize the crown of love
> And scale the mount of heaven."

Moral lessons, bearing on the vanity of life and the constant presence of death, are embroidered. The inscription on Figure 28 represents this grouping. Young children who as yet could not count their years in two figures were obliged to embroider such verses as :

> " Come gentle God, without thy aid
> I sink in dark despair
> O wrap me in thy silent shade
> For peace is only there."

and :

> " There is an hour when I must die
> Nor can I tell how soon 'twill come
> A thousand children young as I
> Are called by death to hear their doom."

The omnipresence of a Vengeful God was kept in mind by lines such as :

> " There's not a sin that I commit
> Nor wicked word I say
> But in thy dreadful book is writ
> Against the judgement day."

Another doggerel which adorned many a garlanded canvas was :

> " Our days, alas, our mortal days
> Are short and wretched too
> Evil and few the patriarch says
> And well the patriarch knew."

Death and the grave were constantly being referred to and samplers were made to serve as funeral cards. Sometimes they bore details of a family tree through several generations ; sometimes a verse commemorated some-one who had just died. The last inscription on Figure 14 is of this category.

A less morbid verse was one which enjoyed wide popularity at the opening of the 19th century though its philosophy was beyond that of the child-workers who embroidered so carefully.

79

FIGURE 28.

Dated 1839. Size 23″ × 26″. Signed Hannah Johnson age 18. Worked throughout in cross stitch in reds and greens. Verse in centre with house trees and animals in solid cross stitch.

FIGURE 29.

Sampler by Gaenor Edwards 1842.

FIGURE 30.
Sampler worked by Sarah Morgan mid 19th Century.

FIGURE 31.
Dated 1866.   Signed Mary Hopper, age 11.   Worked in cross stitch on white canvas in bright colours.
Floral border in green, black and red.

FIGURE 32.

Sampler worked by Margaret Crichton 1853. An example of the work done in a charity school.

" Our life is nothing but a winter's day
  Some only breake their faste and so away
  Other's stay dinner and depart full fed
  The deeper age but sups and goes to bed
  He's most in debt that lingers out the day
  Who dyes betimes has lesse and lesse to pay."

Verses were written in praise of parents and of teachers and were doubtless chosen by them too !

" Dear mother I am young and cannot show
  such work as I unto your goodnefs owe
  Be pleased to smile on this my small endeavour
  I'll strive to learn and be obedient ever."

Another reads :

" Next unto God, dear parents, i address
  Myself to you in humble thankfulnesse,
  For all your Care and Charge on me bestowed
  The means of learning unto me allowed.
  Go on i pray and let me still pursue
  These Golden artes the friendless never knew."

The utterance was at times that of the parent or teacher whereas it was the child who worked the inscription.

" Oh child most dear
  Incline thy ear
  And harken to God's voice
  Return the Kindnesse ye do receive
  As far as ability gives leave."

Acrostic and riddle samplers are met with but only rarely, though in all likelihood these must have had a decided appeal to the child mind. The religious bias given to a child's education resulted in such simple joys being frowned upon and unfortunately children's thoughts were being marshalled strictly in the way it was supposed they ought to go. Wealth and poverty were turned into subjects of child philosophy.

" The World's a City full of Crooked Streets
  And Death's the market place where all men meet.
  If Life was merchandise that Men could buy
  The Rich would live, the Poor alone would die."

Industry was constantly advocated :

> " The busy bee with ceaseless hum
> Morn, noon and evening sucks the flower
> Think you such honey e'er will come
> To those who waste the fleeting hour ? "

A well-known inscription on the same theme was :

The Sluggard.

> " 'Tis the voice of a sluggard I heard him complain
> You have wak'd me too soon I must slumber again.
> As the door on its hinges, so he on his bed
> Turns his sides and his shoulders and his heavy head.
> ' A little more sleep and a little more slumber '
> Thus he wakes half his days and his hours without number
> And when he gets up he sits folding his hands
> Or walks without, sauntring or trifling he stands.
> I passed by his garden and saw the wild brier
> The thorn and the thistle grow higher and higher
> The clothes that hang on him are turning to rags
> And his memory still wastes till he starves or he begs.
> I made him a visit still hoping to find
> He had took better care of improving his mind.
> He told me his dreams, talked of eating and drinking
> But he scarce reads his Bible and never loves thinking.
> Said I then to my heart, ' Here's a lesson for me
> That man's but a picture of what I might be.
> But thanks to my friends for their care in my breeding
> Who taught me betimes to love sewing and working '."

Another verse sorting our virtues and vices reads :

> " Not Land but Learning
> Makes a man complete
> Not Birth but Breeding
> Makes him truly Great
> Not Wealth but Wisdom
> Doth adorn the State
> Virtue not Honour

Makes him fortunate
Learning, Breeding, Wisdom
Get these three
Then Wealth and Honour
Will attend thee."

Self-praise was not regarded as a failing. Sometimes there is present in a verse a smug tone which may have been wholly absent from the children who worked them :

" This needlework of mine may tell
That when a child I learned well ;
And by my elders I was taught
Not to spend my time for nought."

There is redeeming irony in one sampler, slovenly, unkempt, unfinished which bears the inscription :

" This is my Work so
you may see what
care my mother as
took of me."

A couplet frequently worked was :

" Cast but a smile on this my first endeavour
I'll strive to mend and be obedient ever."

One young worker whose sampler is dated 1797 apparently believed that attack is the best form of defence for the inscription reads :

" In reading this if any faults you see
Mend first you own and then find fault in me."

Sewing, reading and writing were constantly extolled as virtues.

" Young ladys faire whose gentle minds incline
To all that's curious, innocent or fine
With admiration in your works are read
The various textures of the twining thread
Then let your fingers with unrivalled skill
Exalt the needle, grace the noble quill."

CHAPTER XII

Map Samplers

MAPS worked as samplers became popular in the latter half of the 18th century. The maps are interesting as forms of decorative needlework and also as showing contemporary ideas on the shapes of the counties and of countries. They reveal in an alarming sense how very little of the New World was known by the common populace even by the year 1777.

That particular date appears with questionable ubiquitiousness on many *objets d'art*. The date is a popular one—no doubt on account of the ease whereby the figures can be worked with the needle which is almost proportionate with that wherewith the date can be inscribed upon a wall with a garden fork!

The map samplers were treasured as specimens of schoolgirl efficiency with the needle and also as testimony of that school lesson termed " the use of the globe."

Not only were map samplers very popular in the latter half of the 18th century but the vogue continued well into the succeeding century. Some maps were worked on satin. The outline of a country was traced upon it in readiness for working and the lines of latitude and longitude were marked clearly together with a north point. Maps thus marked are by far more accurate than those which are not so measured. As examples of handwork, however, those worked without lines and degrees are the most interesting. In the more original work, counties meander at will over the foundation material. While some expand others contract in an alarming fashion and some counties creep out of the picture!

The maps are often set in oval frames whereas the samplers proper are rectangular. The maps show a high standard of lettering. Prominence is given to certain towns by working them in bright colours. It is interesting to observe how a number of towns which were regarded as important when

FIGURE 33.
Map Sampler.

FIGURE 34.
Modern Map Sampler.

the maps were worked have since fallen into decay. The town or village in which the worker lived is sometimes given special attention by elaborate or different lettering. Counties are usually outlined in colour and the name of each is embroidered in black. A floral wreath tied with ribbons often surrounded the map. Figure 33 is an example of a map sampler and Figure 34 is a particularly attractive and exquisitely worked modern interpretation of the theme.

CHAPTER XIII

The Future of the Sampler

IN working a sampler the young pupil learnt mechanical manipulation, certain principles of arrangement and design and studied the units with which to compose design. There was much in sampler work that agreed with modern educational theories in the teaching of the young. Bold and simple designs worked easily and quickly with suitable materials appeal magnetically to the young. Figure 35, is an interesting example of a modern sampler. Further, it has the distinction of being worked by a boy, six-year-old George Martin of Glasgow. The simplicity of the design, the arrangement of the units and the careful workmanship make the sampler particularly attractive and show that sampler work is not effete in teaching the young many useful lessons. Samplers can never be essential again in the social scheme but they represent to the young in particular an aesthetic and manipulative need.

Life has become too heterogeneous for an adult to devote years of careful work to the creating of a sampler. But as a form of decorative needlework the sampler has still a strong appeal.

The sampler work of the Victorian Age wilted because it lacked originality and aesthetic purpose. To survive the sampler must adapt itself to the needs and ideas of the age in which it is worked. The Saga represented on the sampler shown in Figure 37, shows how the modern specimen can adapt itself to be " a thing of beauty and a joy for ever." The tradition of the sampler is worthy of being maintained among those things which form the British heritage.

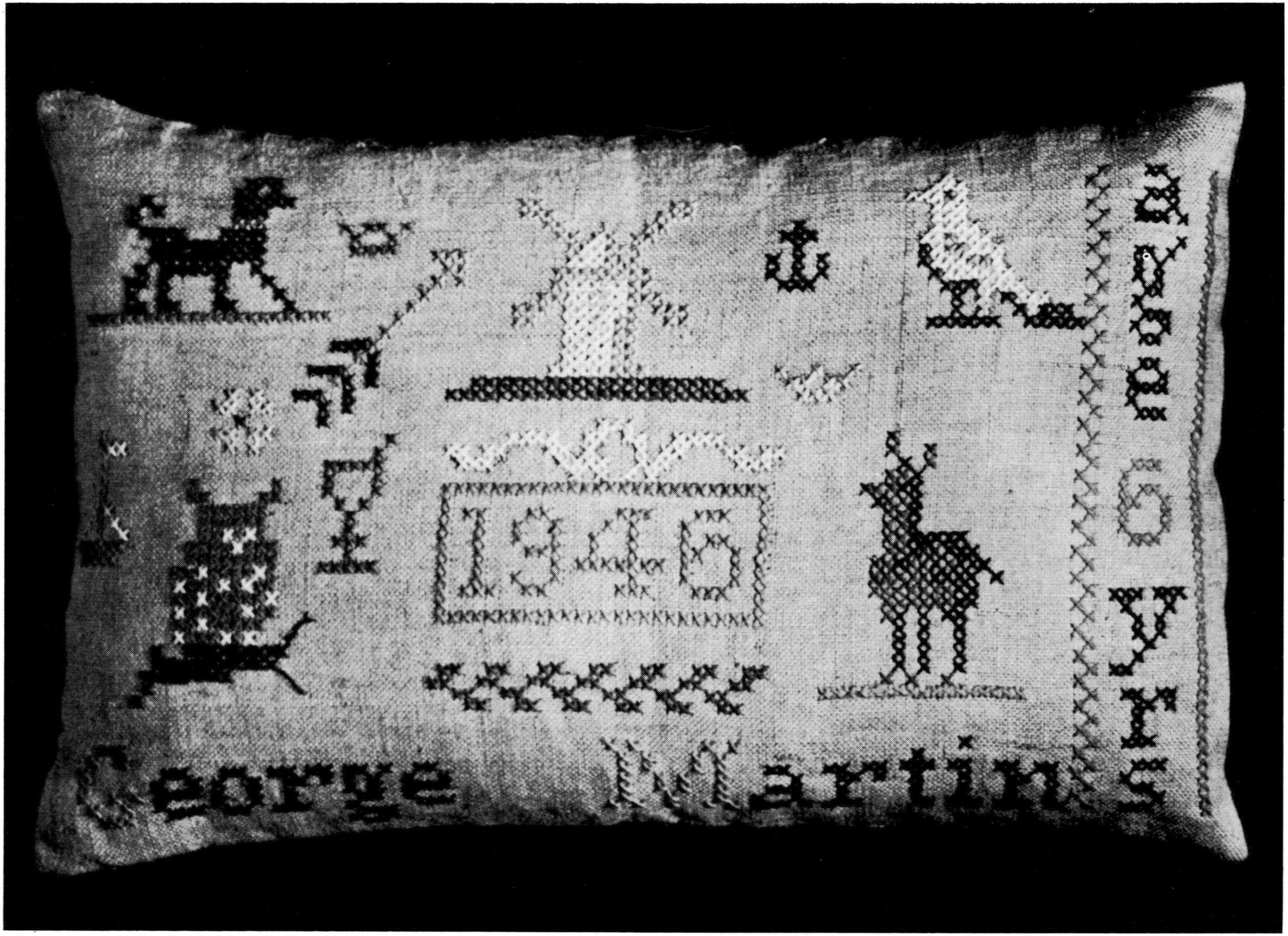

FIGURE 35

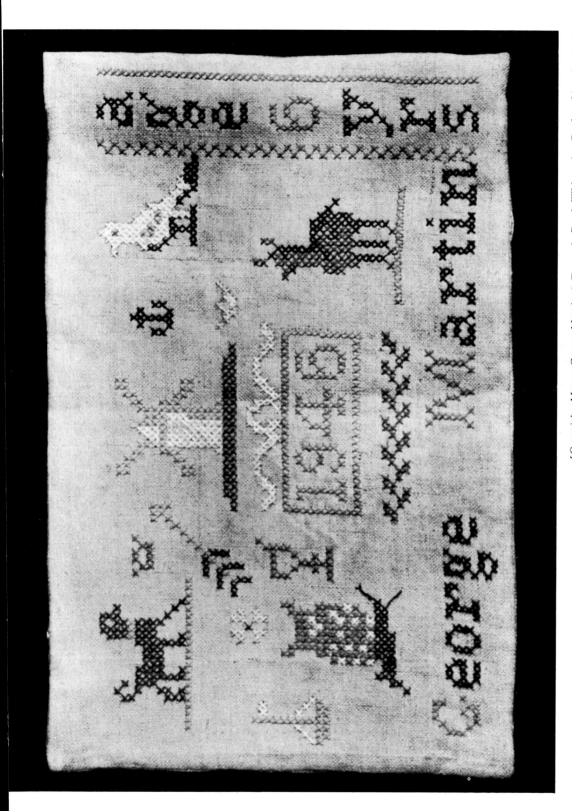

FIGURE 36.

KOHLER SAGA

FIGURE 37.